Nature's Children

PET PARROTS

by Frank Puccio

GROLIER
EDUCATIONAL

FACTS IN BRIEF

Classification of parrots

Class:	*Aves* (birds)
Order:	*Psittaciformes* (parrots)
Family:	*Psittacidae* (parrots)
Subfamilies:	*Cacatuinae* (cockatoos); *Loriinae* (lories and lorikeets); *Psittacinae* (true parrots)
Genus:	Many genera exist, made up of many species.

World distribution. In the wild found mostly in tropical areas. Domestically found everywhere.

Habitat. In the wild, forests and jungles. Domestically need cages, climbing branches, and room for exercise and exploration.

Distinctive physical characteristics. Large head with big beak; reversed toes for climbing and grasping.

Habits. Highly social, with a need to bond with another parrot or parrot substitute; clever; can mimic sounds, even words.

Diet. Grains, vegetables, fruits.

Library of Congress Cataloging-in-Publication Data

Puccio, Frank, 1956-
    Pet parrots / Frank Puccio.
        p.   cm. — (Nature's children)
    Includes index.
    Summary: Presents information on the habitat, physical
characteristics, habits, and diet of parrots, cockatoos, and other
large birds frequently kept as pets.
    ISBN 0-7172-9078-6 (hardbound)
    1. Parrots—Juvenile literature. 2. Cage birds—Juvenile
literature.   [1. Parrots. 2. Birds as pets. 3. Pets.] I. Title.
II. Series
SF473.P3P83   1997
636.6'865—dc21
                                                        97-5980
                                                        CIP
                                                        AC

This library reinforced edition was published in 1997 exclusively by:

Grolier Educational

Sherman Turnpike, Danbury, Connecticut 06816

Set ISBN 0-7172-7661-9
Pet Parrots ISBN 0-7172-9078-6

Contents

What can compare with the sight of a large, beautiful bird flying through the air or landing— brightly colored wings stretched out—on a branch?

Birds, with their colors and flight, have fascinated people for thousands of years. The ancient Egyptians had gods who were birds. The ancient Greeks told tales of daredevils who tried to add wings and feathers to their bodies. And for hundreds of years inventors of all nations worked to create machines that would allow humans to fly like the birds.

Of all the birds of the world few are as colorful and as fascinating as parrots. Beautiful, affectionate, and full of individual personality, they even are clever enough to talk. It's no wonder that for hundreds of years they have been among the world's most treasured pets and companions.

Parrots

What comes to mind when you hear the word parrot? Do you think of a colorful bird calling, "Hello, there!" from a pet store cage? Or do you think of a bright green bird perched on the shoulder of a peg-legged pirate?

Parrots have had an important place in stories and books—especially ones about pirates and adventurers—and they have been popular pets as well. They come, moreover, in all shapes, sizes, and types, from large Amazons to small cockatiels and lovebirds, from colorful macaws to plain African grays.

The colors of their feathers help to hide them from their enemies. They also have large heads and short necks, with short, curved beaks and toes that are reversed for better climbing and grasping. In size they can range from the 4-inch (10.2-centimeter) pygmy parrot of New Guinea to the giant hyacinth macaw, which grows to more than three feet (91 centimeters) in length!

Parrots, like this scarlet macaw, are as beautiful as they are clever.

African Grays

Although its colors are plain, the African Gray is one of the most popular of all pet parrots. The reason is simple: no other parrot comes close to the African Gray when it comes to speaking.

Grays' ability to imitate and speak is quite amazing. They will pick up just about any sound they hear, from a dog's bark to a telephone's ring to a door's creak. They will whistle songs, imitate different people's voices, and actually put words together in sentences. All it takes is time and a patient, careful trainer.

Originally from the forests of Africa, Grays are fairly large birds, about 14 inches (36 centimeters) long. They are very social, and they definitely need company. If a bird is kept alone, it needs to be included in the family's whole range of activities. Left alone in a cage or chained to a perch, it will become so bored that it may pull out its own feathers.

Grays need things to do, too. Playing with toys and chewing on wood are favorite activities. They also need enough room to get plenty of exercise.

The remarkable ability to speak and imitate sounds helps make African Gray parrots the most popular of all.

Macaws

Macaws are another popular member of the parrot family. Unlike African Grays, however, macaws generally are bought more for their bright feathers than their speaking voices.

The truth is, macaws are not great talkers. Birds that are raised by the same person from youth can be taught to speak, but usually only a few words. Some birds never learn to speak at all. This does not mean that they are silent, however. In fact, their voices are so loud and shrill that people say that the sound is like a knife cutting through the air!

Macaws are large, between 18 and 21 inches (46 and 53 centimeters) long. In captivity they do not like to leave their cages much. Therefore their cages should be large enough to let the birds exercise.

Pet macaws get very attached to the people who own them. Usually they will choose one particular person in a household as their special "substitute parrot." Other people are ignored at best; at times a macaw might even treat them with hostility!

Macaws are more famous for their beautiful feathers than for their speaking ability.

How Parrots Come to Us

Even today most parrots bought or sold in North America were originally captured in the wild. Capturing birds, though, is not without problems. Many dealers will stop at nothing to get birds, and they often care little for how the birds are treated on their way to customers. As a result up to half of the birds captured die before they reach their new homes.

To enter the United States legally, every parrot must be inspected by the U.S. Department of Agriculture. Then, if they pass inspection, birds spend 30 days alone, in quarantine, to see if they show any signs of diseases. (Officials are especially concerned that the parrots might bring in diseases that could affect farm birds.)

Once a bird comes out of quarantine, it is given a numbered band. This shows that the bird can come into the United States. For owners this is an important document. It shows that their pet is "legal."

Cockatoos are among the most popular pet birds.

Parrots enjoy companionship so much that they will do just about anything to be with their owners!

Is a Parrot the Pet for You?

All pets are a responsibility. But parrots are more of a responsibility than most.

Parrots are extremely social. Without a lot of companionship they suffer mentally and physically. They even can become physically ill if they are left alone too much.

Ideally a parrot should have another parrot as a companion. But this often is impossible. Luckily parrots usually are able to form a strong bond with something or someone else—often a person. However, this substitute parrot has to be around the pet a great deal of the time.

People thinking about adopting a parrot need to seriously consider this problem. Are they away a lot? Will they have time for their pet?

People also need to realize that parrots are wild birds, not creatures bred for generations to be human companions. It takes understanding and sensitivity to make parrots happy in a human environment. Only if people are sure they can accept this responsibility should they adopt a parrot.

Choosing a Parrot

Before someone chooses a particular bird, he or she should think about what kind of bird to have. Someone, for example, who doesn't have room for a large cage should not get a macaw. That person also should have plenty of room outside the cage where the parrot can walk or fly about. If there isn't enough space, a smaller pet—a cockatiel, lovebirds, or some such bird—would be best.

Once this issue has been decided, choosing becomes a matter of picking the best bird for you. People, of course, should always try to get a healthy bird. Bright, handsome feathers are often a sign of good health. So is lively behavior and a generally calm nature. (A bird, for example, should not necessarily squawk or scream wildly whenever someone approaches its cage.)

It usually is wise to get a young bird. Since so many parrots are captured in the wild, a young bird is more likely to adjust well to people and a new environment. It is also more likely to learn to communicate and talk.

Choosing which parrot is for you can take time—
unless the parrot happens to choose you!

Pretty Cagey

Although almost all domestic parrots have cages of one sort or another, parrots should also be free to wander outside the cage. The exercise and mental activity this provides are absolutely necessary to the birds' health and well being.

Still, parrots need cages, and it is important that these cages provide the correct environment for the birds. First of all they should be big enough. Approximately 39 inches (99 centimeters) high, 27 inches (68 centimeters) wide, and 27 inches (68 centimeters) long is the minimum for a bird the size of an African Gray or a macaw.

The cage also should be made of heavy steel wire so that the bird cannot chew through it. It also should have several sturdy perches as well as containers for food and water.

Finally, the cage should have a tightly fitting door with a strong lock or snap. Parrots are extremely clever and can open most simple latches. Without a secure lock most parrots will find a way to let themselves out of any cage they are put in!

Parrots Need More than a Cage

A cage is just the first step in setting up a good home environment for a parrot. Where the cage is placed is important too.

To begin with, the cage should be in a quiet area of the home, someplace where the parrot can go when it wants to be slightly apart. It also needs to get light without being in direct sunlight. Parrots can suffer from too much heat, so sunny windows as well as radiators or heating vents should be avoided. Drafty windows should be avoided as well.

Parrots also need climbing trees. Climbing trees should have tree branches sturdy enough to hold up to the bird's climbing and perching. These can be purchased at pet stores. But many owners make them by sticking twisted branches into Christmas tree stands or buckets of gravel and sand outside the cage. It is a good idea to have at least one branch reach back to the parrot's cage. That way the bird can walk right into its cage when it wants to!

Parrots are used to being outside where making a mess is not much of a problem.

What a Mess!

Most pets like a clean environment, and parrots are no different. But there is a problem about keeping things clean around a pet parrot. Parrots are messy—really messy.

To begin with, smart, lively parrots will get into everything. They explore and chew, leaving pieces of things behind. They also spill seeds, toss out seed hulls, shed feathers, and give off clouds of dust whenever they peck at or puff out their feathers.

Parrots also are impossible to housebreak. As a general rule they will try not to leave their droppings on their owners or parrot substitutes. But, like seeds and feathers, droppings have a way of getting everywhere.

One possible solution is to keep sheets of plastic over things that can be stained or damaged. But parrots become very much a part of a family and go to many different parts of a home. Because of this it can be difficult to choose what *not* to cover. In the end owners often just decide to live with the cleanup that is part of parrot ownership.

Keeping a Clean Environment

Cleaning up after parrots is quite a job. But if it isn't done often, the birds may get seriously ill.

Any droppings left by a parrot should be cleaned up as soon as possible. If they are not picked up immediately, they should be scraped off as soon as possible. The area then should be washed with warm water. Each day droppings should be spooned out of the grit at the bottom of the cage.

There is other cleaning to do as well. Perches and toys should be cleaned. Droppings must be scraped off and the surfaces scrubbed with warm water. Food and water containers should be washed in hot water each day as well. Then they should be refilled with fresh supplies.

Each week the floor and floor tray of the cage should be cleaned. Scrubbing with a brush and rinsing with clean water is best. Every month the whole cage should be cleaned, wires and all. Hot water—as hot as possible—should be used in order to kill harmful bacteria.

Parrots need a large cage and a way to get outside when they need to exercise.

Birds Like Toys, Too!

Parrots just love toys. Toys give parrots a chance to exercise. They also provide interesting activities. Without toys birds get bored; and, as we've already learned, bored birds can become unhappy and ill.

Toys, however, should be chosen with care. Their size always should match the size of the bird. Giving a small cockatiel a giant toy does the bird no good. Nor will a large macaw appreciate a toy that is too small to handle.

In addition owners should make sure that the toys are not made of harmful substances. Certain plastics can be poisonous. And anything made from nylon fibers can unravel and get wrapped around the birds' feet. This can cut off the circulation of blood and cause permanent injury.

When it comes to toys, wood usually is best. But it should be untreated wood, free of any possibly harmful chemicals. The toys also should be checked for loose parts—bells, clappers, whatever. Anything that can be chewed off or swallowed can become a danger to the bird.

With parrots, when it comes to toys, the more the merrier!

Come and Get It!

Wild parrots find their own food, and they will eat everything from fruits and bark to insects and worms. Domestic parrots, however, depend on their owners for their food. So it is up to their owners to provide a healthful mix of foods.

In general parrots should have a balanced diet of several kinds of foods. One of the most important of these is seed. There are many seed mixes available in pet stores. But owners should carefully read labels to make sure that a particular mixture is good for their pets. They also should experiment to see which one a particular bird likes best.

Seed mixes are only part of the food story for a healthy parrot. Vegetables are needed too. Corn, spinach, radishes, carrots, and lettuce usually are good choices. Fruits also are important. Pears, berries, oranges, grapes, apples, and bananas are among the fruits that parrots often like. Nuts may also be given to the birds, either with or without shells. Parrots also will eat meat. But it is best to keep this to a minimum.

Parrots love treats, especially when they come from an owner's hands.

Can That Bird Really Talk?

Almost every parrot owner is asked this question at one time or another. And just about everyone who wants to own a parrot asks that very same question when he or she goes to choose a bird.

The question of whether—or how much—parrots really talk and understand what they say is something people have been discussing for as long as people have kept parrots. The truth is that parrots are wonderful mimics. They will imitate just about any sounds they hear, including speech. Some will imitate certain words. Others will pick up and repeat whole sentences.

Oddly, though, wild birds rarely imitate any sounds other than those made by other parrots. Even if they live near people, the birds seldom pick up human words or sounds. This has led scientists to believe that domestic parrots mimic and speak as a way to keep busy. It also is a means to communicate with the creatures with whom domestic parrots form their closest bond—people.

In the wild parrots will imitate the sounds other parrots make; in captivity they will imitate just about any sound they hear.

Training

Among parrots the ability to imitate sounds and to speak varies from species to species and even from bird to bird. Some pick up human words almost immediately; others never really master more than just a word or two.

Teaching parrots to speak, regardless of their particular ability, is a matter of repeating the same word again and again and again. Each time the trainer should try to say the words the same way. (Needless to say, it is best to have only one person doing the speech training; otherwise the bird may get confused by the different voices.)

This training takes time and patience. But in time just about any parrot will pick up a word. Once that first word is mastered, most parrots will pick up others much faster.

Speech, of course, is not all that parrots will imitate. Many enjoy whistling songs. Some can master a few notes; others, whole tunes. They even enjoy imitating motions. Many parrots can do fairly good imitations of popular dances.

Parrots can be trained to do tricks as well as to speak!

Grooming

Like most birds, parrots love to keep themselves neat and clean. They spend hours each day working on, or preening, their feathers. All this pecking and biting actually helps arrange their feathers and keep new ones coming in.

In general parrots can take care of their own feathers. But there are a few places they simply cannot reach. Wild parrots have other parrots groom their heads and necks and the underside of their bills. Domestic parrots rely on their substitute parrots for this, so people should be ready and willing to give the birds a "scratch" when it is wanted.

Parrots also need baths. Some like to get right into the water; others like to simply splash around. Still others—African Grays among them—actually prefer a shower! Cage attachments for baths are available in pet stores, and showers can be given through spray bottles. Baths will help a bird and should be given about once a week. On especially warm days some parrots even want to bathe several times, just to keep cool.

Parrots spend hours each day grooming their feathers.

First Aid

Accidents can happen even to the best cared for pet. In some cases a parrot will need care from a trained veterinarian. In others—or until the bird reaches the vet—the pet depends on its owner for first aid.

Breaking a wing or a leg is an unfortunate situation for a parrot, but it is an accident that can happen. When it does, it is important to stop any bleeding that may occur. Gentle pressure in the injured area will do it. As a rule, however, it is best to let a vet actually set or put a splint on the broken limb. The efforts of an untrained person may actually do more harm than good.

This is also true if the bird accidentally eats something that is poisonous or extremely harmful. (This is always a possibility because parrots are so curious and usually have free run of the home.) The bird should be rushed to a vet, and a sample of the substance should be taken along. Again, speedy arrival at the vet will do more than amateur medical help can.

Vets can help parrot owners with check ups and occasional emergency care.

Common Illnesses

Like any animal, parrots will have an illness or two every once in a while. But on the whole, if they are well cared for, they are quite healthy creatures.

An occasional minor illness—sniffles or slight diarrhea—should be no reason to panic. If, however, a bird changes its appearance or behavior in a major way, a vet should be consulted quickly. Some of these changes include red or swollen eyes or droppings of an unusual color. A loss of feathers may also be a sign of illness, as may difficulty in breathing.

Even vets sometimes have difficulty figuring out, or diagnosing, illnesses among parrots. For this reason it is wise to take along a sample of the bird's latest droppings. Many illnesses can be identified by simply testing these droppings.

In particular, owners should be on the lookout for parasites, worms, and mites, all of which can infect parrots. When any of these problems strike, keeping birds apart and thoroughly cleaning and disinfecting cages are immediate steps to take. Beyond this, medications can be prescribed by vets.

Well-groomed feathers often are a sign of a healthy, happy bird.

Breeding

As you have already learned, most domestic parrots have been captured in the wild. Recently, however, attempts have been made to do more domestic breeding of parrots. Although this can be difficult in the long run, it might be a good way to save the lives of the countless parrots who die on the way to pet shops.

Breeding parrots is made more difficult by the fact that you cannot necessarily breed just any pair of birds. Birds have their individual preferences, and sometimes they just won't mate with one another.

Another problem is actually figuring out which birds are male and which are female. Most owners who wish to breed their birds simply put several in a large cage. Birds of opposite sexes will, one hopes, pair up at some time or other. Owners then just have to notice which birds seem to be spending most of their time together!

Once paired, parrots can be encouraged to breed by giving them a cage large enough for flying. They also do better if given plenty of privacy and a diet that is enriched with extra vitamins and minerals.

Wild parrots groom and take care of each other.

Bringing Up Babies

Even when a pair of parrots is encouraged, mating and breeding take time. Owners must learn to be patient. If all goes well, however, the birds will use the nesting box and mate. Then, after a while, eggs will be laid, and three to four weeks after that, they will hatch.

Hatchlings are not anxious to get out into the world. In fact it may take them almost three months to poke their heads out of the box and look at the world outside. During that time they are fed and cared for by the parents. At first it is the female (or hen) that remains with the babies while the male (or cock) brings back food. After a week or so the male starts to feed the babies as well.

Once outside, the young parrots develop quickly. Within two weeks or so they are picking up and eating seeds on their own. At this point they can be put into separate cages. These young birds look very much like their adult parents and relatives, with only slightly darker and duller feathers. Once they go through their first molting (feather shedding), even these differences disappear.

Young parrots like these grow very quickly.

Cockatoos

Cockatoos, which are related to parrots, are a popular pet. Native to the Pacific area—Australia, the Philippines, and Indonesia—they come in several colors and varieties.

In general cockatoos are affectionate but demanding pets, best kept by experienced rather than first-time bird owners. If kept with other birds, cockatoos are highly social. If they are the only bird in a home, they are likely to form strong attachments to people. Unlike some other parrots, however, cockatoos seem to enjoy forming attachments to several people at the same time.

Owners should be aware that cockatoos want to be held and petted often—very often. They enjoy and even need affection. They also need to be kept busy. Without these things they grow unhappy.

Cockatoos are among the best climbers of the parrot family. A good climbing tree is absolutely necessary for them. They also are natural acrobats and enjoy tumbling about.

Cockatiels

Cockatiels, with their peak of feathers and rosy patches on their cheeks, are colorful birds. They also make wonderful pets. Smaller and less demanding than parrots and cockatoos, they are more colorful and more likely to talk than parakeets.

Wild cockatiels originally were found in Australia. But they have been bred in captivity so successfully that cockatiels for sale today are almost always cage-bred birds. They are also extremely intelligent and easily tamed so most people have success when they train them to do tricks or to speak.

Because they have been bred domestically, cockatiels now come in a number of varieties. These range from lutinos, which are almost entirely white or yellow, to cinnamons, which are a silvery tan. Pearling—a type of shading—is also common.

Like parrots, cockatiels also have individual personalities. Some are shy, and some love to come up to complete strangers. Some love to perform, and some prefer to play quietly with toys. Regardless, they are an excellent choice for a pet, even for an inexperienced owner.

Mynah Birds

The mynah is another talking bird, but one that is not related to parrots. In fact mynahs actually are part of the starling family, those small, dark birds that are considered pests by many people!

Originally found in places as far away as Southeast Asia and Hawaii, mynahs have dark brown bodies, black heads and tails, and bright yellow bills and legs.

Like parrots, mynahs have a reputation as mimics and talkers. They also are extremely noisy, and they enjoy making loud screeching sounds. They are particularly noisy at night, just before going to sleep. No one who needs a lot of peace and quiet would ever be happy with a mynah as a pet!

Many people, however, are willing to put up with all this extra noise because of the mynah's amazing ability to speak. Even the best-trained parrot will speak with a slightly screechy quality. Mynahs, however, can imitate human speech almost perfectly. In fact their voices are such accurate imitations of their owners' or trainers' that they are often mistaken for one another!

Mynahs can imitate sounds and speech almost perfectly.

Body Language

Body language is a way of communicating without using words. Among humans a smile welcomes other people, while having arms crossed in front of the chest usually tells others to stand back.

Birds, too, communicate with their bodies. Anything from a loud noise to the sight of a predator can make a parrot, for example, afraid. And most parrots react to fear by pulling their feathers in close to their body—which makes them look extremely skinny.

In contrast, when parrots feel safe, they fluff out their feathers. (They often pull up one of their legs too.) So, in general, a plump, chubby parrot is a happy parrot.

How do parrots show anger? They usually raise their feathers, trying to make themselves look larger than they are. When a parrot spreads out its wings and snaps with its bill, then it is really angry. Many parrots will also give out a loud shriek while they are doing this.

Words to Know

Band A metal or plastic ring, with a label, that identifies a bird; especially a label that states that a bird has passed U.S. Department of Agriculture inspection for import into the United States.

Beak The large, pointed mouth of a bird.

Climbing tree A device made of strong branches on which a parrot or other large bird can perch or climb.

Cock A male bird.

Hatchlings Newly hatched birds.

Hen A female bird.

Molting The shedding of feathers by a bird; birds molt quite regularly.

Perch A place where a bird sits.

Splint Pieces of wood or plastic used to help mend a broken limb.

Substitute parrot A person (or possibly an animal) to which a parrot becomes attached when another parrot is not available.

INDEX

Cover Photo: Ralph Lee Hopkins (The Wildlife Collection)
Photo Credits: Norvia Behling (Behling & Johnson Photography), pages 14, 17, 23, 25, 26, 35, 36, 41; John Giustina (The Wildlife Collection), page 45; Russell R. Grundke (Unicorn Stock Photos), page 8; Martin Harvey (The Wildlife Collection), page 20; Ralph Lee Hopkins (The Wildlife Collection), page 39; Chris Huss (The Wildlife Collection), page 4; Lynn M. Stone, pages 11, 33; SuperStock, Inc., pages 7, 13, 29, 31.